The Complete Christian

Colossians

by

Phillip D. Jensen
&
Tony Payne

St Matthias Press
Sydney • London

The Complete Christian
© St Matthias Press, 1991
Reprinted in this UK edition 1994

St Matthias Press
PO Box 665
LONDON SW20 8RU
ENGLAND
Tel: (081) 947 5686 Fax: (081) 944 7091

ISBN 1 875245 17 0

Typesetting and design by St Matthias Press.

Contents

How to Make the Most of These Studies 5

1   Receiving and Continuing 9
2   Christ Jesus as Lord 17
3   The Great Transfer 23
4   The Apostle of the Worldwide Christ 29
5   Kidnapped 35
6   True Spirituality 41
7   True Spirituality: in the Household 47
8   True Spirituality: in the World 53

How to Make the Most of These Studies

1. WHAT IS AN INTERACTIVE BIBLE STUDY?

These 'interactive' Bible studies are a bit like a guided tour of a famous city. The studies will take you through Paul's letter to the Colossians, pointing out things along the way, filling in background details, and suggesting avenues for further exploration. But there is also time for you to do some sight-seeing of your own—to wander off, have a good look for yourself, and form your own conclusions.

In other words, we have designed these studies to fall halfway between a sermon and a set of unadorned Bible study questions. We want to provide stimulation and input and point you in the right direction, while leaving you to do a lot of the exploration and discovery yourself.

We hope that these studies will stimulate lots of 'interaction'—interaction with the Bible, with the things we've written, with your own current thoughts and attitudes, with other people as you discuss them, and with God as you talk to him about it all.

2. THE FORMAT

Each study contains sections of text to introduce, summarize, suggest and provoke. We've left plenty of room in the margins for you to jot comments and questions as you read. Interspersed throughout the text are two types of 'interaction', each with their own symbol:

Investigate
Questions to help you investigate key parts of the Bible.

Think it Through
Questions to help you think through the implications of your discoveries and write down your own thoughts and reactions.

When you come to one of these symbols, you'll know that it's time to do some work of your own.

3. SUGGESTIONS FOR INDIVIDUAL STUDY

- Before you begin, pray that God would open your eyes to what he is saying in Colossians and give you the spiritual strength to do something about it. You may be spurred to pray again at the end of the study.
- Work through the study, following the directions as you go. Write in the spaces provided.
- Resist the temptation to skip over the *think it through* sections. It is important to think about the sections of text (rather than just accepting them as true) and to ponder the implications for your life. Writing these things down is a very valuable way to get your thoughts working.
- Take what opportunities you can to talk to others about what you've learnt.

4. SUGGESTIONS FOR GROUP STUDY

- Much of the above applies to group study as well. The studies are suitable for structured Bible study or cell groups, as well as for more informal pairs and threesomes. Get together with a friend/s and work through them at your own pace. You don't need the formal structure of a 'group' to gain maximum benefit.
- It is *vital* that group members work through the study themselves *before* the group meets. The group discussion can take place comfortably in an hour (depending on how side-tracked you get!), but only if all the members have done the work and are familiar with the material.

- Spend most of the group time discussing the 'interactive' sections—investigate and think it through. Reading all the text together will take too long and should be unnecessary if the group members have done their preparation. You may wish to underline and read aloud particular paragraphs or sections of text that you think are important.
- The role of the group leader is to direct the course of the discussion and to try to draw the threads together at the end. This will mean a little extra preparation—underlining important sections of text to emphasize, working out which questions are worth concentrating on, and being sure of the main thrust of the study. Leaders will also

probably want to work out approximately how long they'd like to spend on each part.

- We haven't included an 'answer guide' to the questions in the studies. This is a deliberate move. We want to give you a guided tour of Colossians, not a lecture. There is more than enough in the text we have written and the questions we have asked to point you in what we think is the right direction. The rest is up to you. (If you *would* like some additional input, there is a series of tapes available that expound the relevant passages. For details, see the pages inside the back cover.)

5. GETTING STARTED

Before you launch into the first study, it's worth taking time to read right through the letter to the Colossians. It's not very long—it should only take you about 20 minutes. If you are in a group, take it in turns to read 10 verses at a time.

As you read, try to find one or two verses that you think summarize the main thrust of the letter. If you are in a group, you might like to share your ideas and discuss why you think your particular verses are important.

1 Receiving and Continuing

1. A town like Colossae

Imagine, if you can, a fertile valley with a river meandering through it, in what we would now call Turkey. On the shores of the river, at the junction of two important roads, is a town like many 1st Century towns. This is Colossae, just down the road from Laodicea and Hierapolis.

As you stroll through the streets and into the market-place, you encounter a mix of races and religious beliefs—there are Jews there, and Greek mystery religions, and a variety of other cults and religious philosophies. And among the various sub-cultures is a group calling itself 'Christian'.

This group of Christians were the original addressees of the letter that we call 'Colossians' and which we are about to study in some depth.

Let's look briefly at how they came into being and at why the apostle Paul is writing to them.

Investigate

1. What was Paul's relationship with the Christians at Colossae before he wrote to them (see 2:1,5)?

2. Who originally brought the gospel to the Colossians (see 1:6-8)?

3. *What is Paul's description of:*

- *what the Colossians used to be like (1:21; 2:13)?*

- *what they are now like (1:3-8)?*

4. *What is Paul's situation as he writes (4:3,18; cf. Philem 23)?*

We're not certain exactly when the Colossian church came into existence. It may well have been during Paul's lengthy stay in Ephesus (which was not all that far away). In Acts 19, we read that as a result of Paul's teaching in the lecture hall of Tyranus, "all the Jews and Greeks who lived in the province of Asia heard the word of the Lord" (Acts 19:10). Whatever their past history, Paul is delighted with their faith in the gospel, and the fruit of that faith. And he is concerned for their welfare; concerned enough to write to them from his imprisonment.

2. The heresy?

Many people have assumed that Paul was writing to combat a dangerous heresy in Colossae. In chapter 2 of the letter, he certainly gets stuck into somebody or something. However, we need to bear the following things in mind:

- The only information we have about the 'heresy' is that contained in the letter itself. By reading between the lines and taking note of how Paul refutes the heretics, biblical scholars have attempted to reconstruct what the heresy was like.
- No-one seems able to agree on exactly what sort of heresy was involved. There has been a bewildering array of suggestions and perhaps the only thing we can be certain about is that we can't be certain. We don't even know for sure if there was a clearly defined 'heresy'.
- We also need to note that the letter to the Colossians was

meant for a wider audience. In 4:16, Paul urges the Colossians to show their letter to the neighbouring Laodiceans, and in turn to read the Laodicean letter (which we no longer have).

- As every pastor knows, there are always distractions and heresies to lead Christians astray. It is a feature of our sinful world, and it should not surprise us. The Colossian church was by no means unique in having to deal with people or teachings that sought to distract from Christ.
- Finally, we should remember that the Scriptures were written down for *our* instruction. God has inspired Paul's letter to the Colossians so that it speaks to his people in every age, whether they have detailed knowledge of the Colossian 'heresy' or not.

In other words, there may have been a 'Colossian heresy'; it would certainly fit the facts. However, we don't need to worry too much about it. We certainly don't need to know any more about it than Paul actually reveals in his letter. Paul's letter is general enough to be read in other churches (like the Laodiceans') and general enough to apply to us.

Indeed, the striking thing about the false teaching that Paul refutes in chapter 2 is that it is so similar to the kinds of false teaching that abound today. As we look at chapter 2 in more detail later on, we'll see just how much it has to teach 20th Century Christians.

There is much to challenge us in this short but very important New Testament letter, and to get to the heart of that challenge, we are going to leap headfirst into the middle.

3. The Challenge

It may seem rather strange to start studying a letter in the middle, but in Colossians 2:6-7 we find a sentence that virtually summarizes the whole letter:

> So then, just as you received Christ Jesus as Lord, continue to live in him, rooted and built up in him, strengthened in the faith as you were taught, and overflowing with thankfulness.

These two verses are the hinge around which the letter turns. They summarize all that comes before, and outline what is to follow.

In this first study, we will work through these verses almost word by word, and in doing so we'll gain a feel for the message of the whole letter. (In the studies that follow, we'll go back to the beginning and work through the whole letter.)

Investigate

"So then"

The opening two words of these verses prepare the readers for some sort of conclusion. "OK," says Paul, "Given what I have just been saying, this is what I want you to do." What has Paul just been saying?

He has just been reminding the Colossians of his ministry to the Gentiles, of which they are part (1:24-2:5). He has been a servant of the gospel that they have received and has laboured and struggled (with God's strength) to proclaim Christ with the final aim of presenting "everyone perfect in Christ" (1:28).

Even though he has not met the Colossians personally (2:1) he is struggling for them, too. His purpose is that they may know Christ better, and he is delighted to hear that their faith in Christ is orderly and firm.

"just as you received"

So then, says Paul, in light of all that I have been saying, I want you to continue in Christ, *just as you received him*. The word translated 'received' is a special sort of word meaning to have a tradition or body of teaching passed on to you. It's the same word Paul uses in 1 Corinthians 15:1 when he writes: "Now brothers, I want to remind you of the gospel I preached to you, which you *received* and on which you have taken your stand."

What does it mean that the Colossians had "received" Christ? Can you see any clues earlier in the letter? (see esp. 1:3-8, 23)

What do you think is the significance of the two little words "just as" in v. 6?

"Christ Jesus as Lord"

Jesus was a 1st Century Palestinian who was raised in Nazareth, conducted a public ministry throughout Galilee and Judea and was crucified in around 30 AD—that is, around twenty-five years before Paul wrote his letter to the Colossians. Paul calls this Jesus 'Christ'. The word 'Christ' is a title taken from the Old Testament. It means 'anointed one' (the Hebrew word is 'messiah') and describes the ruler or king of Israel. For hundreds of years before the time of Jesus, Israel had not had a king of its own. The Old

Testament prophets looked forward to a time when God would send a great king to liberate Israel from her oppressors and establish a worldwide kingdom. Paul is saying that this Jesus, crucified (and risen) only twenty-five years ago, is that 'Christ'.

What is Jesus Lord of (see 1:13-20)?

"The message of Christianity is a person not an idea." Do you agree? Why? Why not?

"continue to live in him"

In what way were the Colossians to continue their Christian lives?

How do you think this might relate to the false teaching that the Colossians were facing?

"rooted"

The image here is of the Colossians being like a tree whose roots are bedded down in Christ. How does this help us understand the way we are to continue in Christ?

"built up"

The second image is of a building. How (or where) is our 'building' to grow?

"strengthened in the faith"

Here, 'the faith' is the body of teaching or knowledge that the Colossians had received. In what way were they to be strengthened?

"overflowing with thankfulness"

The ongoing Christian life is to be characterized by thankfulness, and lots of it. How is this different from:

human nature

our national character

Summary

To tie it all together, try to re-write Colossians 2:6-7 in your own words (don't use any of the words in the verses, except 'Jesus').

4. Today's message

i Heresy?

We do not know for sure what the Colossian heresy was, or indeed if there was one. But we do know our own world only too well. We know that temptations to turn aside from Christ Jesus the Lord are all around us, and they come in numerous forms.

There are those who tell us that it is juvenile or inconsistent to follow Jesus Christ as the Lord of the world. There are many learned scholars, theologians and ministers who do not regard Jesus as any more than a peculiarly gifted man. For them, he is not the divine ruler of the world, and he certainly did not rise from the dead.

Many of our friends and workmates have the same basic

attitude to Jesus, even if not in such a sophisticated, religious sort of form. They think that Jesus was a good man, even a great man, but they do not allow him to run their lives.

The steady drip of these attitudes can affect us. Even if we have "received Christ Jesus as Lord" like the Colossians, we can easily find ourselves no longer treating him as the Lord—no longer obeying him, and no longer allowing his values and wishes to shape our lives.

We might call this whole problem the 'gospel minus'—that is, *subtracting* Jesus' Lordship from our belief and life.

There is another common way for us to be distracted from continuing in Christ—we might call it the 'gospel plus'. This consists of adding other lords and masters to our lives, thus diminishing the status of Jesus. These other lords can be many and varied. Some people add the church, making its decisions and rules an essential element of the Christian life. "Yes, it's fine to have Jesus as your Lord," they say, "but you must also do what the church/elder/priest tells you."

In the same sort of way, people add the worship of Mary to the gospel, or they require some second blessing of the Holy Spirit, or they add certain kinds of good works (like how to keep the Sabbath). All these are examples of the 'gospel plus'—of adding something to the simple New Testament gospel of 'Christ Jesus as Lord'.

ii Receiving and Continuing

Paul's message to the Colossians was clear. Just as they had accepted Jesus as their Lord, so they were to continue in him— not adding something to him, or wandering off down some other path, or moving on to some higher experience, but growing in the spot where they had been planted: in Christ, the Lord and Master of the Universe.

Think it through

1. Have you received Christ properly—as Lord?

2. *Are you continuing?*

3. *Are you growing?*

4. *What things do you find distract you from Jesus?*

5. *What things tempt you to 'move on' from Jesus?*

2

Christ Jesus as Lord

In the first study, we suggested that Colossians 2:6-7 was a hinge on which the whole letter turned. You might remember that the central idea, or rather the central person, of those two verses was Christ Jesus the Lord—

> So then, just as you received Christ Jesus as Lord, continue to live in him, rooted and built up in him, strengthened in the faith as you were taught, and overflowing with thankfulness.

As we look at Colossians in more detail, we will see that this man Jesus is at the centre of what God is saying in the letter. In particular, Paul argues that Jesus is sufficient; that he is all that the Colossians need, and that it is a fatal mistake to be lured away from him in any way.

1. Who was the Christ?

Whatever else you might say about the motley crowd that call themselves 'Christians', they seem to have one thing in common: an uncommon regard for a Jewish carpenter's son who died nearly 2000 years ago.

Who was he, this Jesus?

In Paul's mind, he was the 'Christ'. Right from the opening greeting in 1:1, Paul identifies himself as an apostle (i.e., messenger) of 'Christ Jesus'. As we've already said in study 1, 'Christ' is an Old Testament term meaning 'anointed one'. This was a Jewish way of saying 'God's king', for that was how kings were chosen and installed—they were anointed with oil (see, for example, the anointings of Saul and David in 1 Sam 9-10 and 16). 'Christ' was not simply Jesus' surname, as if his letters were addressed to Mr J. Christ. It was more of a title, like saying 'King Jesus'.

In the Old Testament, the classic king (i.e., anointed one) was David. It would be a good idea to stop at this point and read a couple of passages that talk about the might of David and that look forward to another 'Christ' like David who would come and save Israel from all their woes.

Investigate (optional)

Look up the following Old Testament passages and jot down what they teach about the 'anointed one' or king that Israel looked forward to?

Psalm 2

Isaiah 11:1-5

Ezekiel 37:24-28

2. The First Extraordinary Fact

As Christians, we are very familiar with the word 'Christ', and we may even be well-versed in its biblical meaning. However, it is easy for us to miss the impact of the statement that Jesus is the Christ.

This is the first extraordinary fact that we come across in the Colossians. Jesus, remember, was a tradesman-turned-prophet who had a following for a short time in Galilee and who was executed by the Jerusalem authorities. He was an obscure man from an obscure part of Palestine who had died an early and humiliating death, seemingly without having achieved any great success.

Yet, in this letter, delivered to some people in Turkey about twenty-five years after his death, Jesus is viewed as the 'Christ'; that is, as God's appointed king of the world, who will judge all the nations of the earth, and rule with justice and righteousness forever and ever. It is an extraordinary claim, especially for a 1st Century Jew like Paul.

Paul sees himself, his colleagues and their relationship with the Colossians, all in terms of this Christ. He is an "apostle of Christ" (1:1) and Epaphras, who first brought them the gospel is a "minister of Christ" (1:7). The Colossians themselves are "holy and faithful brothers in Christ" (1:2) who delight Paul by their "faith in Christ Jesus".

In the course of chapter 1, we find out even more about Christ Jesus, but that's something that you should look up for yourself...

Investigate

Read Colossians 1:1-20.

1. What do you learn about the relationship between Jesus and his Father?

2. What do you learn about who Jesus is? Write down every phrase that tells you something about the person of Jesus and then your own paraphrase of what you think each phrase means.

Verse	Phrase	The meaning in your own words

N.B. The only really tricky bit in chapter 1 is the use of the word 'firstborn' in v. 15 and v. 18. The word refers to an heir or ruler, as in the 'firstborn son' who inherited all the father's property in the ancient world. It is about pre-eminence. In this sense, Jesus is the heir or ruler of all creation (v. 15), as well as the supreme and pre-eminent one in the age of resurrection (v. 18). He is the 'heir' of the age to come.

3. The Second Extraordinary Fact

By now, perhaps, you will have realised that there is a second extraordinary fact in chapter 1 of Colossians. Only twenty-five years after his barbaric death, people are saying that Jesus of Nazareth is the creator, ruler and owner of the entire world; that everything was made by and for him; that he is the exact image and representation of God; and that in him, the entire created order exists and holds together!

That people are even saying this is extraordinary enough; that people are believing and going to prison for it is doubly extraordinary.

Think it through

1. Is it fair to say that Paul regarded Jesus as divine; that is, as God?

2. How does this view of Jesus compare with:

   the common views of people around us?

   your own view?

3. Looking back over what we have covered, write down any questions, comments or insights that you have.

4. Who is in Control?

Paul taught that Jesus of Nazareth was the long-awaited Messiah of Israel. More than that, he insisted that he was God-made-man, that he was the creator and ruler and upholder of the universe. And the Colossians believed it.

In Colossians, this acceptance of the Lordship of Jesus is a vital, personal principle of life. Paul wants the Colossians to lead a life worthy of their Lord, a life that pleases him and bears fruit (1:10). And he reminds them that though once they were alienated from God and lived as his enemies, now they were reconciled to him (1:21-22). They had been transferred from the kingdom of darkness into the kingdom of the Son (1:13).

This is the central issue in Colossians. The Colossians had placed themselves under the Lordship of Christ Jesus. They now lived in a kingdom where he was the king. Would they continue to serve him as their king, or would they allow someone or something else to take his place on the throne?

These are questions we need to think through as well.

Think it through

1. Have you taken the step of submitting to the Lordship of Christ Jesus?

2. If not, what is stopping you?

3. If you were put on trial for having Jesus as your Lord, would there be enough evidence in your life to convict you?

4. Are there areas in which you are consistently failing to submit to Jesus?

3 | The Great Transfer

1. Images of the Ancient World

One of the hardest things about God is finding the right words to describe him. By definition, God is separate from our world and quite distinct; the biblical word is 'holy'. Although we are made 'in his image', he is still different from us in a radical and extraordinary way. How do you precisely describe something (or someone) that is unlike anything in our own world?

The best we can do is use the means that God himself has provided. He has revealed himself to mankind: through Creation and through Israel and finally through Jesus Christ. Throughout his revelation, God uses various images and ideas to describe himself and his relationship with mankind.

In Colossians, we encounter a number of these images. We find the apostle Paul using common words from his own time and culture to describe what God has done for the Colossians. In this study, we'll focus on three short passages and on the images they employ to describe the work of God in our lives—images like dominion, darkness and redemption in 1:13-14; reconciliation, alienation and blood in 1:20-22; and circumcision, legal codes and public humiliation in 2:13-15.

All these images were common in the 1st Century world of Paul and the Colossians. They lived with the reality of kings and despotic rulers, slaves and human bondage, and the unspeakable cruelty of crucifixion. They knew that slaves could be redeemed—that is, freed—by someone paying the right price to the slave-owner.

We need to bear this 'real world context' in mind as we look at these three passages.

2. Our Natural State

Investigate

Read Colossians 1:21-22

1. *What were the Colossians once like? What was their attitude to God?*

2. *How do you think "evil behaviour" affects our attitudes and thought-patterns?*

3. *Do you still perceive this enmity towards God in yourself?*

4. *How do you see it amongst your workmates or friends?*

Read Colossians 1:12-14.

5. *People who reject God tend to think of this rejection as a 'declaration of independence'. What do these verses say about the situation of the Colossians before their conversion?*

Read Colossians 2:11-15.

6. Speaking of spiritual rather than human powers, Paul again reminds the Colossians of what they once were like. What words or phrases does he use to describe their former state?

7. Combining what you have learnt from all three passages, how would you summarise our 'natural' state before we come to know God?

3. How God Acts

It's something of a relief that Colossians does not end on this tragic note. In fact, it focuses on another aspect altogether. Colossians sings with the news that God has not left mankind in this rebellious, enslaved, lost, alienated condition. God does something. Let's investigate the images Paul uses to describe this almost indescribable action.

Investigate

Look again at Colossians 1:12-14.

1. Because of God's actions, the Colossians now have a certain qualification. What is it?

2. How has God done this?

3. In the 1st Century, 'redemption' was how you set a slave free (or made him your slave). You paid a price to his master in order to transfer ownership. How is this image used to describe what God has done?

Re-read Colossians 1:20-22.

4. God has made his enemies into his friends. How has he achieved this? What part does Jesus play in God's action?

Look again at Colossians 2:13-15.

5. Here the imagery is of life and death. Once you were dead, says Paul, but God has made you alive. How has God done this? What needed to be done for us to be raised to new life?

6. We saw earlier that our 'natural' state involves being enslaved to the dark powers of this world. How has God's action changed this? What has God done to the dark powers and how?

4. Where now?

Paul is quite emphatic about it: God has *acted* in Christ Jesus. He has rescued us from one kingdom and transferred us to another; he has qualified us to inherit the kingdom of heaven; he has overcome our alienated hostility and reconciled us to himself in Christ; and he has conquered all the evil powers by cancelling the written code that was their weapon against us.

Paul is emphatic about something else as well. He keeps reminding the Colossians that all this is in the *past* for them. It has been done and has become part of their lives. They *have received* this Christ Jesus as their Lord; they *have been* rescued, redeemed, reconciled and delivered. To go elsewhere, to seek some other sort of path to God, is a terrible blasphemy against what God has already done in Christ. And as we shall see as we look further into chapter 2, Paul is scathing in his criticism of those who have tried to lure the Colossians away from Christ.

All this has implications for us.

Think it through

1. *Looking back over what we've done, do any questions or ideas spring to mind?*

2. *Many people want to keep one foot in each 'kingdom', but this is like trying to keep one foot in two boats, only more difficult. You can only be one or the other: redeemed, reconciled, qualified sons of the kingdom of light; or alienated, hostile, slaves of the kingdom of darkness. What is your state before God? Are you alienated or reconciled? In which 'kingdom' do you live?*

3. Paul's description of mankind's natural state before God is fairly grim. How and where do you see this:

   in our society as a whole?

   among your friends, workmates, family?

4 The Apostle of the Worldwide Christ

So far in our study of Colossians, at least one thing should have become clear—that 2:6-7 is a key passage in the argument of the letter:

> So then, just as you received Christ Jesus as Lord, continue to live in him, rooted and built up in him, strengthened in the faith as you were taught, and overflowing with thankfulness.

Colossians is not so much about *becoming* a Christian as *continuing* a Christian. Paul urges the Colossians to stick with Christ, and he musters strong language to make the point.

They had received Jesus as their Messiah and Lord (not, notice, as their brother or friend or even just saviour). He is the Creator of all, the Ruler of the living and the dead, and they were not to go beyond him. They were not to seek God elsewhere as if he could be found in further secret knowledge or in mystical experiences. Like a strongly rooted tree or a firmly founded building, they were to grow and be strengthened in *what they had been taught* (i.e., not in some new teaching or emphasis).

This seems a fairly straightforward point, and one which may not seem to need a lot of elaboration. However, Christians in every age have found this difficult. There always seems to be someone saying things like:

"Yes, I know you've received Christ as your Lord but
   ...are you going to the right church?
   ...are you using the right translation of the Bible?
   ...have you received a second blessing?
   ...do you have these particular gifts of the Spirit?"

In Colossians, God has a stark reminder for us: as we have received Christ, so we must continue to live in him. If we have received him as our Lord, then we must continue to live with him as our Lord.

This continuity between our original acceptance of Christ and our ongoing life in him is expressed throughout Colossians. In this study, we'll see how it comes out in Paul's description of his *prayers* and his *ministry*. We'll look at each of these in turn, and see how fixated Paul was with Christ and his gospel. It comes out in almost everything he says and does.

1. The Apostle at Prayer

Investigate

Paul had a habit of starting his letters with a thanksgiving prayer, and his letter to the Colossians is no exception. He tells the Colossians how he had been thanking God for them and praying for their growth.

Read Colossians 1:3-14.

1. What two things in the lives of the Colossians does Paul thank God for?

2. On what are these two things based?

3. Where did they hear of this?

4. The word 'gospel' keeps cropping up in this passage. Essentially, it means 'news'—news that is good or bad depending on how you take it! From these verses, what is the 'news'?

5. In vv. 9-14, Paul moves on to tell the Colossians about what he has been praying for. Lots of points are listed, but if you look closely there is only thing that Paul asks God to give the Colossians. What is it?

6. He prays this with particular, long-term goals in mind. What are they?

Knowing God's Will

"May we all be filled with the knowledge of his will"—so goes the Christian chorus, and so also goes a welter of theories and ideas about the importance of 'knowing God's will for your life'.

Many 20th Century Christians use the phrase 'knowing God's will' to mean knowing God's direction for particular decisions. "I sense that it's God's will for me to become a Christian _____" in which the blank space is filled by words like 'musician', 'doctor', 'film-maker' or 'businessman', but rarely by words like 'street sweeper' or 'factory hand'. It seems that God's will often runs along middle-class lines and tends up-wards.

Alternatively, the phrase is used to describe a knowledge or sense of God's presence in our lives. To be filled with a knowledge of God's will seems, for many people, to imply being in touch with God's power; discerning his presence in our daily lives and walking according to his directions.

But note Paul's use of the phrase in this passage. 'Knowing God's will' means knowing how to please God, and to live a life worthy of all that he is and all that he has done for us. It means bearing fruit by doing good works; it means knowing God better; it means being strengthened to endure when things aren't going so well, and patiently and joyously thanking God for his saving grace.

This doesn't sound very spectacular by 20th Century spiritual standards, but it is what God wants. In comparison, nothing else matters.

Think it through

1. What does it mean to "know God's will"?

2. How do we gain this knowledge?

3. How does this relate to our key verses (in 2:6-7) about continuing on in Christ?

4. Write down any other questions, comments or insights that have come to mind.

2. The Apostle at Work

As chapter 1 proceeds, Paul moves on to talk about his own life and work as God's apostle to the Gentiles. This is important in the flow of the letter, because it establishes an important principle. It shows that Paul's focus on Christ, and his desire that the

Colossians continue in Christ, was not just something that he held intellectually and urged upon others. It was something that pervaded his own life, not only in his prayers, but also in the day to day exercise of his ministry. Paul had been commissioned by God to a remarkable work—to take the news about the universal Lord Jesus to people of every nation. With this sort of commission (and this sort of Lord), we can begin to see why Paul saw the impossibility of there being any alternative to Christ.

Investigate

Read Colossians 1:21-23.

1. What do the Colossians have to do in order to be found holy in God's sight, "without blemish and free from accusation"?

2. What is Paul's part in this?

Now read Colossians 1:24-2:5.

3. As Paul describes something of his life and ministry, what do we learn about:

how he became involved in the work of the gospel (1:25; cf. 1:1)?

what day to day life is like in his ministry (1:24, 29; 2:1)?

the content of his message (1:26; 2:2)?

his aims (1:28; 2:2-5)?

Think it through

1. *Paul's ministry focused on seeing people from all the nations of the world grow to maturity in Christ. To this end, he taught, proclaimed, admonished and prayed. It was the aim of his life—is it the aim of yours? In what ways would having this aim:*

shape your own life?

affect the way you relate to others?

2. *Do you pray to this end for yourself and those around you? Why is it important to pray for this?*

5 Kidnapped

1. Christians Under Threat

In our last study, we saw how Paul wanted the Colossians to keep going in Christ. He longed for them to grow to maturity in their knowledge of God, and he prayed hard and worked hard to this end.

Paul was particularly concerned about the Colossians, because he knew there were alternatives to Christ being touted in their midst. Even though he was delighted by their firm and orderly faith (2:5), he was still concerned about the threat that they were facing. In the passage we'll focus on in this study, we'll see just how severe this threat was, and how equally severe Paul was in his denunciation of it.

So far in the letter, Paul has reminded the Colossians of their immediate past history. They had received Christ Jesus as their Lord (study 2), been rescued by him from the kingdom of darkness (study 3), and were steadily and firmly growing to maturity (study 4). He summarizes all this in our (by now) familiar verses in 2:6-7.

> So then, just as you received Christ Jesus as Lord, continue to live in him, rooted and built up in him, strengthened in the faith as you were taught, and overflowing with thankfulness.

In 2:8f, Paul turns directly to the danger that is threatening the Colossians. They are in danger of losing their way, of wandering off in the wrong direction—more than that, they are in danger of being captured and carried off.

> See to it that no-one takes you captive through hollow and deceptive philosophy, which depends on human tradition and the basic principles of this world rather than on Christ.

Like Christians in every age, the Colossians were in danger of being kidnapped or 'taken captive'. Someone was suggesting that there was more to Christianity than receiving Christ Jesus as

Lord (and growing in him). There was a next step, or an alternative step, or a series of rules or practices to be followed—and these were supposedly the path to a higher, fuller, deeper knowledge of God. These teachers stood in judgement over other members of the Colossian church, seeking to disqualify or condemn anyone who didn't follow their teachings (see 2:16, 18).

Paul's answer was uncompromising—this alternative philosophy was a step *back* to captivity, not forward to some deeper knowledge. The false teachers promised much, but lacked substance. Their philosophy was hollow, deceptive and of human, not divine, origin.

In 2:9-23, Paul gives examples of this "hollow and deceptive philosophy". Let's look at these examples, and how he refutes them, before turning to how we are threatened today.

Investigate

Read Colossians 2:8-23

We may not be too sure about the details of the 'deceptive philosophy' that the Colossians were facing, but it seems that spiritual 'powers and authorities' played an important part in it. Paul's opponents may well have taught that these spiritual powers stood between God and man, almost as a buffer. By pleasing or placating these spiritual powers, mankind could press past them into the very presence of God and to a new level of spiritual experience (Peter O'Brien suggests this in his short but excellent book *Understanding the Basic Themes of Colossians, Philemon*, page 72). Whatever their precise role, the spiritual powers of the universe were obviously seen as being of some importance to the Christian life.

1. According to Paul, where did the Colossians stand with regard to these 'powers and authorities'? And why?

2. *The false teachers were urging the Colossians to observe certain religious practices, as a way of progressing spiritually. Fill in the following table, showing Paul's answer to these practices and (if you can) some 20th Century equivalents.*

	verses	Paul's answer	modern equivalents
circumcision			
austere regulations (about food/drink etc)			
religious festivals			

3. *These practices, especially the denial of food and drink, and the harsh treatment of the body, were deemed effective for gaining visions and other mystical experiences. What is Paul's attitude to this?*

2. A Never-Ending Story

The false teaching that faced the Colossians sounds rather exotic, with its emphasis on circumcision and harsh treatment of the body, its promise of mystical visionary experiences, and its strange doctrines about angels and spiritual powers. It sounds quite removed from our 20th Century world.

However, the sad truth is that false teaching of this kind has plagued Christianity in every century, including our own. There have always been false teachers urging Christians to take on a load of rules and regulations in addition to Christ.

We don't have many teachers championing circumcision today, but we have plenty of religious leaders who insist that some external, ritual 'badge' is necessary in order for us to be true members of Christ's church. It might be baptism (sprinkled, sprayed or dunked), or confirmation—depending on which denomination you would like to choose. In each case, they are saying (in effect) that receiving Christ Jesus as Lord is not sufficient; having a certain quantity of water come in contact with your skin is also necessary.

There is also confusion in some circles about the application of the Old Testament law—the Seventh Day Adventists, for example, have a long history of legalism over the observance of the Sabbath.

Today, as in the 1st Century, religious people insist that some days are inherently more holy than others. The Seventh Day Adventists, throughout most of their history, have maintained that Christians must observe Saturday as an Old Testament style sabbath in order to be acceptable to God. Along the same lines, there are those who would place restrictions on what Christians should eat and drink, whether in the traditional mode (no alcohol, no meat on Friday) or in the more modern, trendy mode (no white sugar, no white rice, no red meat, no caffeine).

All this gives the appearance of great religiosity, just as it did in the Colossian church 1900 years ago. But it is as empty and useless now as it was then. The kingdom of God does not consist of food and drink, but of righteousness, peace and joy in the Holy Spirit (Rom 14:17). "Nothing outside a man can make him 'unclean' by going into him," said Jesus. "Rather it is what comes out of a man that makes him 'unclean'" (Mk 7:15).

But the most dangerous modern counterpart of the Colossian 'problem' is the increasing tendency to seek a mystical/visionary experience of God apart from or beyond Christ. There are 'Christian' leaders around today who promise a deeper, fuller spirituality based on visions, special worship, and other mystical techniques. Such teachers are open to the same severe criticism that Paul levels at the Colossian false teachers—they have lost connection with the Head, that is, with Christ. Rather than growing and being strengthened in the one true gospel, they advocate a new emphasis or a missing dimension that supposedly offers the key to a higher life.

The challenge for us is the same as it was for the Colossians—to see to it that we, too, are not taken captive by hollow and deceptive ideas based on human traditions and wisdom.

Think it through

1. Look back over the material in this study. Do any questions or issues spring to mind?

2. In what ways have you experienced or come in contact with teaching that fits the description we've been looking at in this study?

3. Are there subtle rules or regulations in your church/fellowship that threaten to become an addition to the gospel?

6 True Spirituality

1. The Positive Alternative

'Spirituality' is a buzz word these days. Everyone, and not only Christians, is looking for the secret of a deeper, more vibrant 'spiritual life'. Even within the broad Christian spectrum there are lots of alternatives on offer—from revamped mediæval mysticism to thinly disguised versions of Eastern philosophy.

In our last study, we saw how an alternative 'spirituality' was threatening to captivate the Christians at Colossae. Paul was scathing in his criticism. The combination of harsh physical discipline, exotic worship and religious rules were of absolutely no spiritual value, according to Paul. They did not open the way to a deeper experience of heaven (as someone at Colossae seemed to be claiming).

In this study, we look at the positive alternative. Having demolished the spiritual credentials of the opposition, Paul teaches the Colossians about true spirituality. The false teachers claimed to be very 'heavenly' and high-minded. They offered the key to a deeper, more profound knowledge of God and eternity. In chapter 3, Paul proceeds to give his own version of what constitutes 'heavenly' or 'spiritual' living.

Investigate

Colossians 3:1-4 is an important passage in the flow of the letter. It is a 'hinge' between Paul's strong attack on the false teachers in 2:8-23 and his positive instruction about Christian living in 3:5-4:6.

Read Colossians 3:1-4.

1. Paul makes some important statements about the Colossians and where they stand with God—some things happened decisively in the past, some are present realities, and some lie in the future. List these statements in the following table and see if you can summarize them in your own words:

	verse	statement	in your own words
Past			
Present			
Future			

2. In light of these facts, what should the Colossians DO?

Although Paul's opponents claimed to be very spiritual and interested in heavenly mysteries, their teaching was earth-bound. It was 'according to the basic principles of this world' (2:8, 20). In 3:1-4, Paul directs the Colossians to be 'heavenly minded' in a true and Christ-centred way.

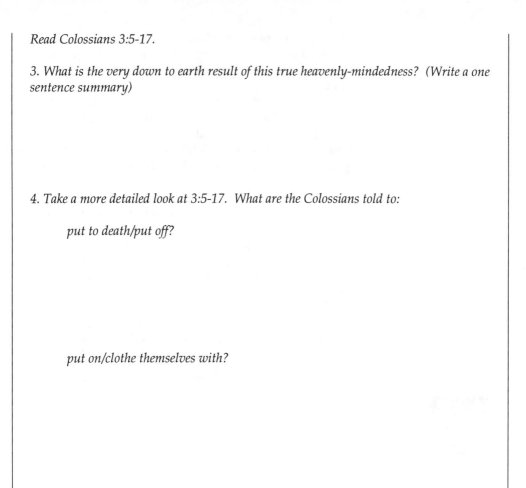

Read Colossians 3:5-17.

3. What is the very down to earth result of this true heavenly-mindedness? (Write a one sentence summary)

4. Take a more detailed look at 3:5-17. What are the Colossians told to:

    put to death/put off?

    put on/clothe themselves with?

2. A Focus on Heaven

This passage in Colossians 3 is one of the most challenging in the New Testament. In it, we read of the positive Christ-centred alternative to deceptive, empty human spirituality. God has some mind-stretching, life-changing truths to teach us about where we are in Christ and what the Christian life is about.

Paul reminds the Colossians that they are living in the overlap of the ages. There has already been a decisive change. Their old sinful personality has died with Christ on the cross. It is dead and gone, and they have been raised with Christ to God's right hand in heaven. Their life is now truly hidden with Christ in heaven. And yet they still live on earth and struggle with the vestiges of the earthly nature that died with Christ on the cross.

This overlap between the 'already' and the 'not yet' crops up throughout the New Testament. In Christ, we are *already* forgiven and made righteous. We have a place in heaven and we simply await its consummation. However, that consummation has *not yet* happened. We still wait for it, and struggle to put to death our old bad habits and clothe ourselves with the characteristics of heaven.

How different this is from the false spirituality of Paul's opponents—and which continues to dog Christians to this day. We still are confronted, as Paul was, with spiritual teachers who offer novel techniques and teachings as the means to a higher (or deeper) life with God. And like the Colossians we should not be fooled. True spirituality, true contact with heaven, true knowledge of the Eternal God—these things all belong to the ordinary Christian. And how? Because we have been united with Christ, in whom all these things dwell in abundance. We should focus our whole beings on Christ, and put to death whatever is inconsistent with our union with him (i.e., ungodly thoughts, behaviour, attitudes). In fact, it reminds us of some other familiar words:

> So then, just as you received Christ Jesus as Lord, continue to live in him, rooted and built up in him, strengthened in the faith as you were taught, and overflowing with thankfulness.
>
> Colossians 2:6-7

Think it through

1. Is the glorious status that is described in this passage yours? Have you died with Christ and been raised with him to the very presence of God?

2. If so, is that where your mind is fixed? Is it your longing, your desire, the focus of your life?

3. *As Paul spells out the practical ways this heavenly focus is lived out, which things strike you as being things you need to work on? In practical terms, what is:*

something you need to get rid of?

something you need to become?

7 True Spirituality— in the Household

1. A Spirituality for the Kitchen Sink

Our last study ('True Spirituality') concluded with a broad demand for our lives to be dominated by the Lordship of Jesus:

> And whatever you do, whether in word or deed, do it all in the name of the Lord Jesus, giving thanks to God the Father through him.
>
> Colossians 3:17

In Colossians 3:1-4, Paul wrote of the true spirituality (or 'heavenly mindedness') that comes from knowing Christ, in contrast to the hollow and deceptive spirituality being taught by the false teachers. True spirituality is shown in putting off and putting on—that is, putting off all that belongs to our old selves and putting on the characteristics befitting God's holy, beloved children. True spirituality is a life in which everything is done in the name of the Lord Jesus (3:17). This leads naturally on to the section we'll be looking at in this study (3:18-4:1). The Lordship of Christ is to change every aspect of our lives—it is not about deep, esoteric mysteries, but about everyday relationships.

The teaching in 3:18-4:1 is cast in the form of a 'household code'. In the ancient world, codes of household rules were relatively common, in which the responsibilities or duties of different members of the house (or of society generally) were outlined. Paul's household code is similar in some ways to these other ancient codes—but there are some important differences, particularly in the motivation behind the code and the demands it places on *all* members of the household (cf. other ethical codes of this kind in Eph 5-6; 1 Pet 3; Tit 2).

As we turn to this passage, we need to recognise that we may find some of its teaching hard to stomach. The values and attitudes of our society often conflict with the Bible, and nowhere more controversially than in relation to the roles of men and women. Amidst this conflict, it is easy to become very negative about obeying God. Instead of reading his word in order to find new ways to please him, we find ourselves reading it *extra* closely to find a loophole. At some point in our study of these verses, we will have to deal with this conflict of values in a way that fulfils the overall thrust of the passage—that is, that we might do everything in the name of the Lord Jesus.

Investigate

Read Colossians 3:18-4:1

1. What commands are given to:

Wives	Husbands
Children	**Parents/Fathers**
Slaves	**Masters**

2. Now list all the phrases in the passage which contain the words 'Lord' or 'Master'.

verse	phrase

verse	phrase

3. In light of this, what is the connection between 3:17 and 3:18-4:1?

4. "Paul's commands in this section of Colossians have been largely determined by the culture of the 1st Century. They therefore have very limited relevance for 20th Century Christians."
Do you agree? Why? Why not?

2. God's Pattern

In your investigation of this passage, you would have seen a pattern emerging. In each of the three sets of commands, there were reciprocal obligations. Wives must submit and husbands must love; children must obey and fathers must teach. This pattern of roles is a feature of the Bible's teaching about our relationships.

There has been a great deal of controversy about this 'pattern' of relationships and roles, and in this short space we cannot do more than touch on some of the issues. Some people have argued that the patterns of submission Paul teaches here (and in other places) are determined by the culture of the 1st Century and are thus inapplicable to 20th Century Christians.

However, it seems much more likely, upon a close reading of the relevant parts of the Bible, that it is *our* culture that is the problem rather than Paul's. The idea of 'submission' is anathema to many modern Western Christians, but why is this? Many of us have swallowed the worldly idea that 'freedom' and 'rights' equal the absence of any restraint or authority. The feminist movement has added to the confusion by promoting the idea that equality and justice for women can only be achieved by uniformity. These ideas run deep within us, but they don't originate in the mind of God—they are the fruit of our society's 200-year slide away from a Christian way of looking at things.

For Paul, "lumbered with his primitive 1st Century culture", the pattern of submission and loving leadership was part of the way God created the world. In almost every sphere of life, Paul seems to suggest, God has created us to fill certain roles—roles which do not depend on any inherent superiority, but on our relationship with the other person. And in living out these roles in a godly way, we are living a life of true spirituality. It is an example of doing "everything in the name of the Lord Jesus" (3:17).

Think it through

1. If you are married, how do you think Paul's commands in vv. 18-19 should work out in practice?

2. In what ways can parents—especially fathers—embitter their children?

3. Is there a point at which the obligation to obey our parents ceases? Does the obligation to honour our parents ever cease (cf. Eph 6:1-3)?

4. How do the principles of slaves/masters apply to our work situations?

5. How does this contrast with the attitudes of most wage-earners in our society?

6. If we are in charge of others at work, what practical steps can we take to treat them rightly and fairly?

8 True Spirituality— in the World

In studies 6 and 7, we looked at Paul's positive alternative to the false teaching at Colossae. We characterised it as 'true spirituality', as opposed to the false and deceptive spirituality of Paul's opponents. We could summarize it as follows:

Investigate

Read Colossians 4:2-18

1. In 4:2, Paul urges the Colossians to be "watchful and thankful"—watchful for what and thankful for what? (Remember the context going back to 3:1-4.)

2. What does this passage teach us about:

the nature of prayer (vv. 2, 12-13) ?

the content of prayer (vv. 3-4, 12)?

3. What are Paul's obligations regarding evangelism (vv. 3-4)?

4. What are the Colossians' obligations regarding evangelism (vv. 2, 5-6)?

5. What do you think it means for our conversation to be "full of grace, seasoned with salt" (v. 6)?

In this last section of the letter, some important themes emerge about the work of the gospel. We could summarize them under the following headings:

1. Prayer

The really striking reference to prayer in these verses is mentioned almost in passing by Paul. He reassures the Colossians that their friend and brother Epaphras is "always wrestling in prayer for you" (v. 12). Prayer is hard work. It is something that Paul encourages the Colossians to 'devote' themselves to—i.e., it's not something that comes to them naturally or spontaneously. They had to work at it, consciously and deliberately.

It is also interesting to see how the work of the gospel and prayer go hand in hand in Paul's mind. Both he and Epaphras pray long and hard for their friends in Colossae; he asks them to pray for his ministry; and he urges them to pray for their own ministry to outsiders.

2. Evangelism

In these verses, we also see Paul the proclaimer, looking for an opportunity to spread the message of Christ. We've already seen (in 1:28) that this was the essence of his ministry—

> We proclaim [Christ], admonishing and teaching every-
> one with all wisdom, so that we may present everyone
> perfect in Christ. To this end I labour, struggling with all
> his energy, which so powerfully works in me.

Now he asks the Colossians to pray that a door might be opened so that he can continue his task of preaching the message.

There is a slight difference, however, between the role of the apostle and the role of the Colossian Christians. Paul's role was to proclaim, to stand in the city square and preach, to *make* opportunities. That was his commission from God. The Colossians were engaged in the same great enterprise, but their task was slightly different. They were to interact wisely and graciously with their neighbours and make the most of opportunities as they arose. If Paul's job was to *make* opportunities, theirs was to *take* opportunities.

Perhaps we should not press this distinction too hard, but it is a useful model for evangelism. There will also be some individuals who are given to the church as 'evangelists'. We aren't all gifted in this area, but we *are* all obliged to act wisely towards non-Christians and to make the most of opportunities that come our way. We are to cultivate conversation that is kind and gracious and yet which is "seasoned with salt". The reference to 'salt' implies a sparkling, interesting, challenging brand of conversation that leads towards the gospel of Christ. As Peter puts it: "Always be prepared to give an answer to everyone who asks you to give the reason for the hope that you have. But do this with gentleness and respect" (1 Pet 3:15).

3. Partnership

Finally, the theme of 'partnership' runs through this passage. Paul, Epaphras, Tychicus, Paul's other colleagues, the Colossians themselves—they are all partners in the one momentous cause. The task of proclaiming Christ is multi-faceted. It is not the job of one gifted individual.

In his final greetings, we glimpse something of the teamwork and partnership that characterized Paul's ministry. We see the mutual prayer support, encouragement and sharing of news. We see the comfort he derives from his immediate friends amidst struggle and hardship. We even see something of the wider fellowship of Christian churches, as the Colossians are encouraged to swap letters with the Laodiceans (whose letter is now lost).

Think it through

1. Colossians 4:2 contains a direct command from God—that we devote ourselves to prayer. Could your prayer life be described as 'devoted', or have you given up keeping watch? What practical steps could you take to obey the command of God here?

2. How might this passage affect the content of your prayers?

3. What do you think would constitute wise behaviour towards outsiders?

4. What steps could you take to render your conversation more 'gracious and salty'? Do you know how to explain the gospel to someone? Does God ever get a mention in your daily conversation?

Also from St Matthias Press

In the Interactive Bible Study series...

BEYOND EDEN (GENESIS 1-11)

The first eleven chapters of the Bible are full of cataclysmic events—the creation of the world, the fall of mankind, the flood. But what is their significance for 20th (soon to be 21st) Century Christians? Looking back at Genesis from this side of Christ, what are we to make of it? *Beyond Eden* leads you on a voyage of discovery to find life-changing answers to these questions. Authors: Phillip Jensen and Tony Payne, *Price £3.50*

THE GOOD LIVING GUIDE (MATTHEW 5:1-12)

The Beatitudes are among the best-known verses in the Bible, but have you ever taken the time to find out what they really mean? *The Good Living Guide* unlocks the treasures of the Beatitudes by going back to the Old Testament. The Old Testament was Jesus' Bible, and all of the Beatitudes are either direct quotes from it or strongly reflect its teaching. *The Good Living Guide* will not only help you discover afresh the meaning of Matthew 5:1-12, it will teach you how to understand the New Testament by learning the message of the Old. And most importantly of all, you will have the painful but exhilarating experience of being challenged by the words of Jesus. Authors: Phillip Jensen and Tony Payne, *Price £2.95*

THE PATH TO GODLINESS (TITUS)

Down the centuries, Christians have suffered from the effects of two damaging (and opposite) problems. There always seem to be people wanting to impose rules and regulations for Christians to follow. On the other hand, there have always been Christians who seem not to care about how they live, and who regard God's forgiveness as a blank cheque. How can we avoid these problems and be motivated to live a life pleasing to God? If the idea of "being Godly" is attractive, how can we turn our vague yearnings into a reality? Titus reveals th3e answers — warning of the false trails and giving stirring encouragement about the source of true Godliness. *Price £1.95*

CASH VALUES: FIVE STUDIES ABOUT MONEY

Money is a subject we get easily embarrassed about, so much so, in fact, that we rarely sit down to carefully work out what God has to say about it. Cash Values is designed to help us do just that. In a series of short, thoroughly readable studies, Tony Payne guides us through the important Bible passages about money. We discover God's attitude to the rich and the poor, the importance of paying what we owe, and what it means to be partners in giving. Straightforward and punchy discussion blended with responsible attention to the Scriptures makes Cash Values a valuable resource for both churches and individuals. *Price £2.50*

THE LEADERSHIP PAPERS

The nine sessions that make up this training programme in basic Christian doctrine are designed to provoke thought and discussion about the fundamental truths of Christianity. Each one is based on a statement from a standard evangelical doctrinal basis of faith. The Leadership Papers are suitable for any Christian who wants to sharpen their understanding of Biblical truth, but as the name suggests, they are especially intended for people who have any potential for Christian leadership, or are involved in teaching in the church. *Price £3.95.*

KEEP IT FREE: GALATIANS

What happens when Christians disagree about something as fundamental as the relationship between law and grace? They write a letter about it - at least Paul did. Galatians is God's answer to the raging debate over rules and regulations that does not seem to go away. The eight chapters of Keep it Free unlock the sometimes convoluted arguments of Galatians, and challenges us to face up to the 20th Century versions of those who would add works to the grace that has been poured out on us in Jesus Christ. *Price £2.95.*

THE ONE AND ONLY: DEUTERONOMY

With Israel poised on the edge of the promised land, God speaks to them through Moses. But what do you say to a nation which has a record of not listening? How can they be persuaded to live a life worthy of the mercy God has shown them? Will they respond to Moses charge to love God with everything they've got?

Deuteronomy is, on the one hand, a story of a people: their laws, their lives, their hopes and their dreams. But it is supremely about their God, Yahweh, the creator of the universe, the One and Only. This new 8-session study guide explores Deuteronomy through New Testament eyes. It leaves us with a picture of an awesome and wonderful God who has kept his promises and, in his Son, delivered salvation to his worldwide people, as we sit on the edge of our heavenly inheritance. *Price £3.25.*

TWO CITIES: ISAIAH

Two Cities is designed to help us get a grip on – and to grip us with – the message of Isaiah. It cuts a highway through the 'branches', 'stumps' and 'deserts' and takes us to where the road forks - to the City of destruction and the City of God. Careful explanations of difficult passages and well-crafted, challenging questions make studying this crucial Old Testament book a whole lot less daunting. Ideal for both individual and small group study. *Price £3.25.*

Colossians on Tape

For those who would like some further input on Colossians, a set of tapes is available which expounds the passages looked at in *The Complete Christian*. These seven sermons by Phillip Jensen provide additional insights and ideas, and tie the material together in a way that is possible in a sermon, but not in a group Bible study.

The tapes are an ideal accompaniment to these studies, especially for group leaders who want to do some additional preparation.

Cost for the full set of seven tapes (including postage to anywhere in the UK) is £10.50. To place your order, phone us on (081) 947 5686 or write to the address below. Enclose a cheque with your order or, if you prefer, we can invoice you.

St Matthias Press
PO Box 665
LONDON SW20 8RU
ENGLAND

TELL US WHAT YOU THINK OF
THE COMPLETE CHRISTIAN

The Complete Christian is the third in a series of Interactive Bible Studies. We'd like your comments and feedback so that we can continue to improve them as we go along. Please fill in the following questionnaire after you have completed the studies and return it to:

St Matthias Press, PO Box 665, LONDON SW20 8RU

1.　We don't want to know your name, but could you tell us your:

sex _____ age _____ denomination _____

2.　Are you a full-time Christian minister?

❒　yes　　　　❒　no

3.　Did you do the studies:

❒　by yourself
❒　with one or two others
❒　with a group of 5-10 others
❒　with a group of more than 10

4.　Did you find the level of the studies:

❒　too low/simplistic
❒　about right
❒　too high-brow/intellectual

5.　Did you feel that the studies were practical enough in their application?

❒　yes　　　　❒　no

6.　How long, on average, did each study take to work through (individually)?

_____

7.　If you did the study in a group, how long, on average, did you spend discussing each one?

_____

8.　Do you have any comments or suggestions about individual studies?

Study no. 　Comment

_____
_____
_____
_____

9.　Do you have any overall comments or suggestions?

_____
_____
_____